# WORLD'S TOUGHEST TONGUE TWISTERS

by **JOSEPH ROSENBLOOM**
drawings by DENNIS KENDRICK

**Sterling Publishing Co., Inc.   New York**

To Sondra Cohen

**Library of Congress Cataloging-in-Publication Data**

Rosenbloom, Joseph.
  World's toughest tongue twisters.

  Includes index.
  Summary: An illustrated A-Z compilation of some of
the world's toughest tongue twisters including
"'Twixt six thick thumbs stick six thick sticks" and
"Truly rural, Truly rural, Truly rural."
  1. Tongue twisters.  [1. Tongue twisters]
I. Kendrick, Dennis, ill.  II. Title.
PN6371.5.R616  1986      818'.5402      86-5983
ISBN 0-8069-4802-7
ISBN 0-8069-4803-5


ISBN 0-8069-6596-7 (pbk.)

## Books by Joseph Rosenbloom

Biggest Riddle Book in the World
Daffy Definitions
Doctor Knock-Knock's Official Knock-Knock
    Dictionary
Funniest Joke Book Ever!
Funniest Riddle Book Ever!
Funniest Knock-Knock Book Ever!
Funny Insults & Snappy Put-Downs
Gigantic Joke Book
Knock-Knock! Who's There?
Looniest Limerick Book in the World
Mad Scientist
Monster Madness
Nutty Knock Knocks
Ridiculous Nicholas Haunted House Riddles
Ridiculous Nicholas Pet Riddles
Ridiculous Nicholas Riddle Book
Silly Verse (and Even Worse)
696 Silly School Jokes & Riddles
Wacky Insults and Terrible Jokes
Wild West Riddles & Jokes
Zaniest Riddle Book in the World

# Before You Begin

How do you say a tongue twister correctly? There are two rules. First, tongue twisters must be said fast. You can say any tongue twister without stumbling if you say it slow enough. The trick is to say it fast—the faster the better.

The second rule is that most tongue twisters need to be repeated a certain number of times. If the tongue twister is several sentences long—let's say, the size of a paragraph—you only need to say it once in order to succeed (but remember to say the words fast!).

If the tongue twister is just one or two short sentences long, get through it twice without making a mistake and you have succeeded.

If the tongue twister is less than a sentence long, say it at least three times. (Those short tongue twisters are listed three times in this book.)

The tongue twisters in these pages have been chosen because they are hard to say. In fact, they include all the toughest tongue twisters in the world—or, anyway, the toughest ones I could find. (I also slipped in a few that weren't so tough, but that were so funny or so great to say that I couldn't resist them.)

Why pick such tough tongue twisters? Because the tougher they are, the funnier they are. Turn to any page in this book and you'll find your tongue doing ridiculous things. It will slip, slide, hesitate, get thick, get thin, and finally tangle up completely, and that's fun. It makes you laugh.

Try them out. Better yet, ask your friends to try them. Why not share the fun?

Ape cakes, grape cakes.
Ape cakes, grape cakes.
Ape cakes, grape cakes.

If I assist a sister-assistant, will the
sister's sister-assistant assist me?

"What ails Alex?" asks Alice.

Andrea and Andrew ate eight acid apples accidentally.

The little addled adder added ads.

Abe and Babe will grab a grub from Greg.
Will Abe and Babe grab a grub from Greg?
If Abe and Babe will grab a grub from Greg,
Where's the grub from Greg Abe and Babe
       will grab?

Ann Anteater ate Andy Alligator's apples, so angry Andy Alligator ate Ann Anteater's ants.

Can an active actor always actually act accurately?

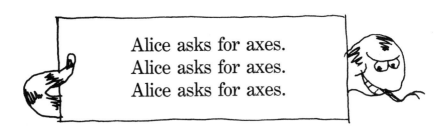

Alice asks for axes.
Alice asks for axes.
Alice asks for axes.

Once upon a barren moor
There dwelt a bear, also a boar,
The bear could not bear the boar,
The bear thought the bear a bore.
At last the bear could bear no more
That boar that bored him on the moor.
And so one morn he bored the boar—
That boar will bore no more!

## The Bold Bald Bear

Who bit the bold bald bear on the shoulder on the boulder and made the bold bald bear on the boulder bawl?

A big bug bit a bold bald bear and the bold bald bear bled blood badly.

Blake the baker bakes black bread.

Bring the brown baked bread back.

Betty Botter bought a bit of butter.
"But," said she, "this butter's bitter.
If I put it in my batter,
It will make my batter bitter.
But a bit of better butter—
*That* would make my batter better."
So Betty Botter bought a bit of better butter
(Better than her bitter butter)
And she put it in her bitter batter
And made her bitter batter a bit better.

The bottom of the butter bucket is the buttered bucket bottom.

"The bun is better buttered," Buffy muttered.

A bachelor botched a batch of badly baked
    biscuits.
Did the bachelor botch a batch of badly
    baked biscuits?
If the bachelor botched a batch of badly
    baked biscuits,
Where are the badly baked biscuits the
    bachelor botched?

A box of biscuits, a box of mixed biscuits, and a biscuit mixer.

I bought a bit of baking powder and baked a batch of biscuits. I brought a big basket of biscuits back to the bakery and baked a basket of big biscuits. Then I took the big basket of biscuits and the basket of big biscuits and mixed the big biscuits with the basket of biscuits that was next to the big basket and put a bunch of biscuits from the basket into a biscuit mixer and brought the basket of biscuits and the box of mixed biscuits and the biscuit mixer to the bakery—and opened a can of sardines.

A big blue bucket of blue blueberries.

Blue beads in a blue rattle rattle blue beads.

Billy's big black-and-blue blister bled.

The big bloke bled in the big blue bed.

Bobby Bear's B-B bean shooter.
Bobby Bear's B-B bean shooter.
Bobby Bear's B-B bean shooter.

The best breath test tests breath better.

Bright bloom the blossoms on the brook's
bare brown banks.

The bleak breeze blights the brightly
blooming blossom.

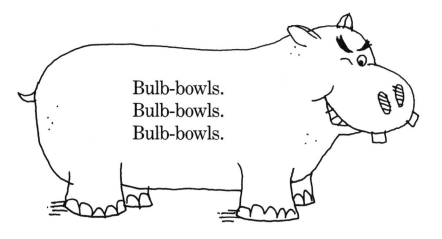

Bulb-bowls.
Bulb-bowls.
Bulb-bowls.

The fuzzy bee buzzed the buzzy busy
beehive.

The bootblack brought the black boot back.

The bootblack blacks boots with a big
blacking-brush.

Blair's blue boots are beauties.

A brave maid sat on her bed braiding broad
braids.
"Braid broad braids, brave maid! Braid
broad braids, brave maid!"

I have a black-backed bath brush. Do you
have a black-backed bath brush?

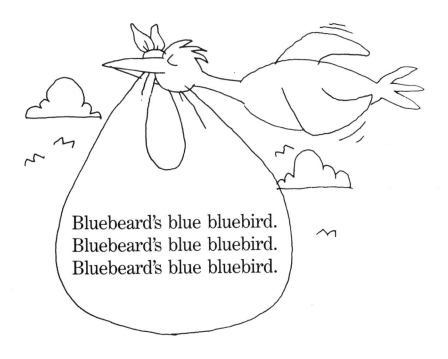

Bluebeard's blue bluebird.
Bluebeard's blue bluebird.
Bluebeard's blue bluebird.

Bluebirds in blue birdbaths.

The brave bloke blocked the broken back bank door.

The boy blinked at the blank bank blackboard.

Bland Bea blinks back.
Bland Bea blinks back.
Bland Bea blinks back.

Pass the big black blank bank book back. If you won't pass the big black blank bank book back, then pass the small brown blank bank book back.

Bertha blocked the bleached back beach benches.

Biff Brown bluffed and blustered.

Bob bought a bleached blue-beaded blazer.

Bess is the best backward-blowing bugler in the Boston brass band.

Three blind mice blew bugles.

Betty Block blows big black bubbles.

Betty Block bought bright bric-a-brac.

A big black bat flew past.
A big brown bat flew past.
Did the big black bat fly past faster than the
    big brown bat flew past?

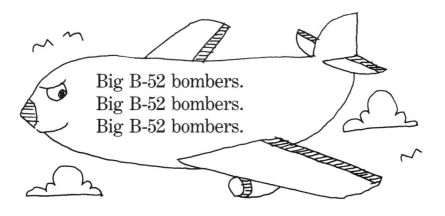

Big B-52 bombers.
Big B-52 bombers.
Big B-52 bombers.

The blunt back blade is bad.

Ted Blake's back brake-block broke a
    bearing.
Did Ted Blake's back brake-block break a
    bearing?
If Ted Blake's back-brake block broke a
    bearing,
Where's the bearing Ted Blake's back
    brake-block broke?

Bill had a billboard.
Bill also had a board bill.
The board bill bored Bill,
So Bill sold his billboard
And paid his board bill.
Then the board bill
No longer bored Bill,
But though he had no board bill,
Neither did he have his billboard!

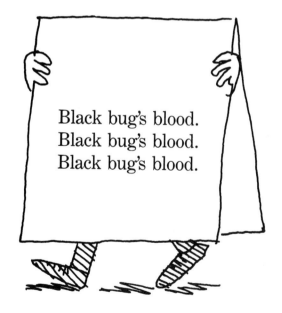

Black bug's blood.
Black bug's blood.
Black bug's blood.

Red bug's blood, bed bug's blood.

Borrowed burros bring borrowed barrels.

A bitter biting bittern
Bit a better brother bittern,
And the better bittern bit the bitter biter
     back,
And the bittern, bitten
By the better biting bittern,
Said, "I'm a bitten bitter biting bittern,
     bitten better now, alack!"

Clean
clams
crammed in
clean cans.

A canner exceedingly canny,
One morning remarked to his granny,
  "A canner can can
  Anything that he can,
But a canner can't can a can, can he?"

Catch a can canner canning a can as he does
the cancan, and you've caught a can-canning
can-canning can canner!

New cheese, blue cheese, chew cheese please.

Top chopstick shops stock top chopsticks.

Where can I find a cheerful cheap chop suey shop?

Cheerful Charlie chose a cheesy chowder.
Did cheerful Charlie choose a cheesy
      chowder?
If cheerful Charlie chose a cheesy chowder,
How cheerful was Charlie after he chose the
      cheesy chowder?

A chapped chap chopped chips.

Cuthbert's cufflinks.
Cuthbert's cufflinks.
Cuthbert's cufflinks.

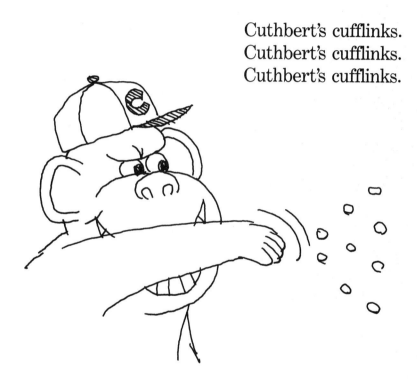

A cheeky chimp chucked cheap chocolate chips in the cheap chocolate chip shop.

The fish-and-chip shop's chips are soft chips.

Does this shop stock cheap checkers?

How much caramel can a canny cannibal
cram in a camel, if a canny cannibal can
cram caramel in a camel?

Chester shucked the chestnuts and Chuck
    chucked the shucks.
Did Chester shuck the chestnuts faster than
    Chuck chucked the shucks,
Or, did Chuck chuck the shucks faster than
    Chester shucked the chestnuts?

The cute cookie cutters cut cute cookies.
Did the cute cookie cutters cut cute cookies?
If the cute cookie cutters cut cute cookies,
Where are the cute cookies the cute cookie
      cutters cut?

A cupcake cook in a cupcake cook's cap cooks
cupcakes.

Crisp crust crackles.
Crisp crust crackles.
Crisp crust crackles.

Choice chilled cherries cheer Cheryl.

All I want is a proper cup of coffee,
Made in a proper copper coffeepot.
You can believe it or not—
I want a cup of coffee
In a proper coffeepot.
Tin coffeepots or
Iron coffeepots,
They're no use to me.
If I can't have a
Proper cup of coffee
In a proper copper coffeepot—
I'll have a cup of tea!

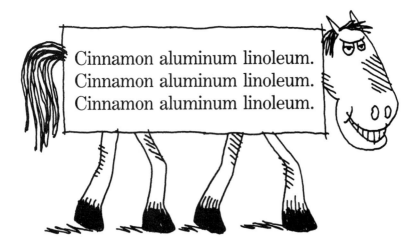

Cinnamon aluminum linoleum.
Cinnamon aluminum linoleum.
Cinnamon aluminum linoleum.

If Sue chews shoes, should she choose to
chew new shoes or old shoes?

If a good cook could cook cuckoos so fine
And a good cook could cook cuckoos all the
time,
How many cuckoos could a good cook cook
If a good cook could cook cuckoos?

A curious cream-colored cat crept into the
crypt and crept out again.
Did the curious cream-colored cat creep into
the crypt and creep out again?
If the curious cream-colored cat crept into
the crypt and crept out again,
Where's the curious cream-colored cat that
crept into the crypt and crept out
again?

Who checked the chart of the cud-chewing cow?

If you must cross a course cross cow across a crowded cow crossing, cross the cross coarse cow across the crowded cow crossing carefully.

A clipper shipped several clipped sheep.
Were these clipped sheep the clipper ship's
    sheep,
Or just clipped sheep shipped on a clipper
    ship?

Charles chose the chief cheap sheep section.

Cheap sheep soup.
Cheap sheep soup.
Cheap sheep soup.

"Cheep-cheep," chirped the cheery chick.

I do like cheap sea trips,
Cheap sea trips on ships.
I like to be on the deep blue sea,
When the ship she rolls and dips.

As I was dashing down Cutting Hill,
A cutting through the air
I saw Charlie Cutting sitting
In Oscar Cutting's chair,
And Oscar Cutting was sitting cutting
Charlie Cutting's hair.

If you cross a cross across a cross,
Or cross a stick across a stick,
Or cross a stick across a cross,
Or cross a cross across a stick,
Or stick a stick across a stick,
Or stick a cross across a cross,
Or stick a cross across a stick,
Or stick a stick across a cross,
What a waste of time!

Great crates create great craters, but great craters create greater craters.

Can Claire cue Carl's curtain call?

A cricket critic cricked his neck at a critical cricket match.

I would if I could.
If I couldn't, how could I?
I couldn't if I couldn't, could I?
Could you if you couldn't, could you?

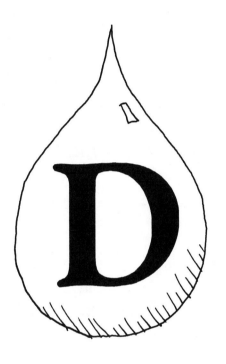

Do drop in
at the
Dewdrop Inn.

How much dew could a dewdrop drop if a
dewdrop did drop dew?

When a doctor gets sick and another doctor doctors him, does the doctor doing the doctoring have to doctor the doctor the way the doctor being doctored wants to be doctored, or does the doctor doing the ˙ doctoring of the doctor doctor the doctor as he wants to do the doctoring?

Does double bubble gum dubble bubble?

The duke dropped the dirty double damask dinner napkin.

Down the deep damp dark dank den.

Diligence dismisseth despondency.

My dame had a lame, tame crane;
My dame had a lame, tame crane.
Oh, pray, gentle Jane,
Let my dame's lame crane
Pray drink and come home again.

A dozen dim ding-dongs.
A dozen dim ding-dongs.
A dozen dim ding-dongs.

A maid with a duster
Made a furious bluster
Dusting a bust in the hall.
When the bust it was dusted
The bust it was busted,
The bust it was dust, that's all.

Elegant elephants.
Elegant elephants.
Elegant elephants.

Esau Wood would saw wood. Oh, the wood that Wood would saw! One day Esau Wood saw a saw saw wood as no other wood-saw Wood ever saw would saw wood. Of all the wood-saws Wood ever saw saw wood, Wood never saw a wood-saw that would saw like the wood-saw Wood saw would. Now Esau saws wood with that wood-saw he saw saw wood.

Eight eager eagles ogled old Edgar.

Edgar at eight ate eight eggs a day.

Ere her ear hears her err, her ears err here.

Did you eever iver ever in
    your leaf loaf life
See the deevil divil devil
    kiss his weef wofe wife?
No, I neever niver never in
    my leaf loaf life
Saw the deevil divil devil
    kiss his weef wofe wife.

I saw Esau kissing Kate.
Fact is, we all three saw.
I saw Esau, he saw me,
And she saw I saw Esau.

For fine fresh fish, phone Phil.

For French shrimp, try a French shrimp shop.

Freckle-faced Freddie fidgets.

The fickle finger of fate flips fat frogs flat.

Five frantic frogs fled from fifty fierce
fishes.

Five fifers free,
Fifing in the fog,
Phyllis, Fran
And Phil and Dan
And Philip's funny frog.

Try fat flat flounders.
Try fat flat flounders.
Try fat flat flounders.

A lively young fisher named Fischer
Fished for fish from the edge of a fissure.
  A fish with a grin
  Pulled the fisherman in.
Now they're fishing the fissure for Fischer!

Francis fries fresh fish fillets.

Frank feasted on flaming fish at the famous Friday fish fry.

Can a flying fish flee far from a free fish fry?

Flat flying fish fly faster than flat flying fleas.

Fried fresh fish,
Fish fried fresh,
Fresh fried fish,
Fresh fish fried,
Or fish fresh fried.

Fran feeds fish fresh fish food.

A fish-sauce shop's sure to sell fresh fish sauce.

## A Flea and a Fly

A fly and a flea in a flue
Were imprisoned, so what could they do?
  Said the fly, "Let us flee!"
  "Let us fly!" said the flea.
And they flew through the flaw in the flue.

Said the flea to the fly as he flew through
    the flue,
"There's a flaw in the floor of the flue."
Said the fly to the flea as he flew through
    the flue,
"A flaw in the floor of the flue doesn't
    bother me.
Does it bother you?"

A fly fled fat Flo's flat.
A flea fled fat Flo's flat.
Did the fly or the flea flee fat Flo's flat first?

Five fat French fleas freeze.
Five fat French fleas freeze.
Five fat French fleas freeze.

Few free fruit flies fly from flames.

Feed the flies fly food, Floyd!

The furry fly flitted from flower to flower.

### Friendly Bugs

Friendly fleas and fireflies.
Friendly fleas and fireflies.
Friendly fleas and fireflies.

Friendly fleas and huffy fruitflies.
Friendly fleas and huffy fruitflies.
Friendly fleas and huffy fruitflies.

False Frank fled Flo Friday.

Flee from fog to fight flu fast.

Fifty-five flags freely flutter from the floating frigate.

Free flag.
Free flag.
Free flag.

Four fliers flip-flop.
Four fliers flip-flop.
Four fliers flip-flop.

Four free-flow pipes flow freely.

I'd rather lather Father
Than Father lather me.
When Father lathers
He lathers rather free.

Fancy Nancy didn't fancy doing fancy work.
But Fancy Nancy's fancy aunty did Fancy
    Nancy doing fancy work.
So Fancy Nancy did fancy work for Fancy
    Nancy's fancy aunty.

Five flashy flappers
Flitting forth fleetly
Found four flighty flappers
Flirting flippantly.

Three fluffy feathers fell from Phoebe's
flimsy fan.

Flighty Flo Fisk and frisky Fritz Fisk.

Of all the felt I ever felt
I never felt a piece of felt
That felt the same as that felt felt
When I first felt that felt.

Menu

Fine fresh fodder.
Fine fresh fodder.
Fine fresh fodder.

A fat-free fruit float.
A fat-free fruit float.
A fat-free fruit float.

A fine field of wheat,
A field of fine wheat.

Greek grapes.
Greek grapes.
Greek grapes.

Gus goes by Blue Goose bus.

Granny's gray goose goes last.

Great gray geese graze gaily daily.

Three gray-green greedy geese,
Feeding on a weedy piece,
The piece was weedy,
And the geese were greedy,
Three gray-green greedy geese.

Good gunsmoke, bad gunsmoke.
Good gunsmoke, bad gunsmoke.
Good gunsmoke, bad gunsmoke.

Good blood, bad blood.

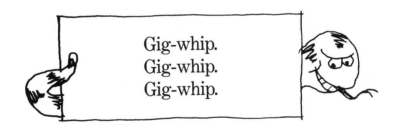

Gig-whip.
Gig-whip.
Gig-whip.

Cows graze in droves on grass that grows on grooves in groves.

Gale's great glass globe glows green.

The glum groom grew glummer.

The cruel ghoul cooks gruel.

Glum Gwendolyn's glasses.
Glum Gwendolyn's glasses.
Glum Gwendolyn's glasses.

Higgledy-Piggedly!
Higgledy-Piggedly!
Higgledy-Piggedly!

Heed the head henpecker!

Horrible Heidi hears hairy Horace holler.

High roller.
Low roller.
Lower a roller.

PSSSST!

The hare's ear heard ere the hare heeded.

How much hair could a hairnet net,
If a hairnet could net hair?

Harry Hunt hunts heavy hairy hares.
Does Harry Hunt hunt heavy hairy hares?
If Harry Hunt hunts heavy hairy hares,
Where are the heavy hairy hares Harry
Hunt hunts?

Hurry, Harry!
Hurry, Harry!
Hurry, Harry!

"Hello, Harry Healy!" hollered Holly
Hartley.

## Hottentot Tots

If a Hottentot taught
A Hottentot tot,
To talk ere the tot could totter,
Ought the Hottentot tot
Be taught to say "ought,"
Or what ought to be taught her?

If to hoot and to toot
A Hottentot tot
Was taught by a Hottentot tutor,
Should the tutor get hot
If the Hottentot tot
Hoots and toots
At the Hottentot tutor?

In Huron, a hewer, Hugh Hughes,
Hewed yews of unusual hues.
Hugh Hughes used blue yews
To build sheds for new ewes;
So his new ewes blue-hued ewe-sheds use.

How hollow Helen Hull hobbles on hills!

Hiccup teacup!
Hiccup teacup!
Hiccup teacup!

A haddock!
A haddock!
A black-spotted haddock!
A black spot
On the black back
Of a black-spotted haddock!

I see Isis's icy eyes.

Ike ships ice chips in ice chips ships.

Can you imagine an imaginary menagerie manager imagining managing an imaginary menagerie?

Our Joe wants to know if your Joe will lend our Joe your Joe's banjo. If your Joe won't lend our Joe your Joe's banjo our Joe won't lend your Joe our Joe's banjo when our Joe has a banjo!

A gentle judge judges justly.

James jostled Jean while Jean jostled Joan.

June sheep sleep soundly.

Kinky kite kits.
Kinky kite kits.
Kinky kite kits.

Nutty Knott was not in.
Nutty Knott was out
Knotting knots in netting.
Nutty Knott was out,
But lots of knots
Were in Nutty Knott's knotty netting.

A knapsack strap.
A knapsack strap.
A knapsack strap.

Keenly cleaning copper kettles.
Keenly cleaning copper kettles.
Keenly cleaning copper kettles.

Come kick six sticks quick.

Knee deep, deep knee.
Knee deep, deep knee.
Knee deep, deep knee.

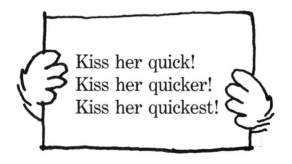

Lanky Lawrence lost his lass
and lobster.
Did Lanky Lawrence lose his lass
and lobster?
If Lanky Lawrence lost his lass
and lobster,
Where's the lass and lobster Lanky
Lawrence lost?

Lonely lowland llamas are ladylike.

Let lame lambs live.
Let lame lambs live.
Let lame lambs live.

Lisa laughed listlessly.

Larry sent the latter a letter later.

Literally literary.
Literally literary.
Literally literary.

Lester lists the lesser lesson last.

Lesser leather never weathered lesser wetter weather.

Red leather!
Yellow leather!

A lump of red leather.
A red leather lump.

He who laughs last laughs last.

Lemon lime liniment.
Lemon lime liniment.
Lemon lime liniment.

Little licorice lollipops.
Little licorice lollipops.
Little licorice lollipops.

Mummies munch much mush;
Monsters munch much mush;
Many mummies and monsters
Must munch much mush.

Moses supposes his toeses are roses;
But Moses supposes erroneously;
For nobody's toeses are poses of roses
As Moses supposes his toeses to be.

GOOD MORNING,
THIR!

Miss Smith lisps as she talks and lists as she walks.

"Are you aluminiuming, my man?"
"No, I'm copperbottoming 'em, mum."

I miss my Swiss Miss.
My Swiss Miss misses me.

The minx mixed a medicine mixture.

A missing mixture measure.
A missing mixture measure.
A missing mixture measure.

Menu

Much mashed mushrooms.
Much mashed mushrooms.
Much mashed mushrooms.

Nick knits Nixon's knickers.

I need not your needles,
They're needless to me,
For the needing of needles
Is needless, you see.
But did my neat trousers
But need to be kneed,
I then should have need
Of your needles indeed.

Ninety-nine knitted knick-nacks were nicked by ninety-nine knitted knick-nack nickers.

Nine nimble noblemen nibbled nuts.

Nippy Noodle nipped his neighbor's nutmegs.
Did Nippy Noodle nip his neighbor's
     nutmegs?
If Nippy Noodle nipped his neighbor's
     nutmegs,
Where are the neighbor's nutmegs Nippy
     Noodle nipped?

Ned Nott was shot and Sam Shott was not.
So it's better to be Shott than Nott.
Some say Nott was not shot, but Shott
    swears he shot Nott.
Either the shot Shott shot at Nott was not
    shot or Nott was shot.
If the shot Shott shot shot Nott, Nott was
    shot.
But if the shot Shott shot shot Shott himself,
Then Shott would be shot and Nott would
    not.
However, the shot Shott shot shot not Shott
    but Nott.
It's not easy to say who was shot and who
    was not,
But we know who was Shott and who was
    Nott.

There's no need to light a night light
On a light night like tonight;
For a night light's just a slight light
On a light night like tonight.

Nine nice night nymphs.
Nine nice night nymphs.
Nine nice night nymphs.

"Nighty-night, knight," said one knight to the other knight the other night. "Nighty-night, knight," answered the other knight the other night.

Oliver Oglethorpe ogled an owl and oyster.
Did Oliver Oglethorpe ogle an owl and
    oyster?
If Oliver Oglethorpe ogled an owl and oyster,
Where's the owl and oyster Oliver
    Oglethorpe ogled?

"Under the mother otter," uttered the other otter.

Awful old Ollie oils oily autos.

The owner of the Inside Inn
Was outside his Inside Inn,
With his inside outside his Inside Inn.

An oyster met an oyster,
And they were oysters two;
Two oysters met two oysters,
And they were oysters too;
Four oysters met a pint of milk,
And they were oyster stew.

Peter Piper picked a peck of pickled peppers.
A peck of pickled peppers Peter Piper
    picked.
If Peter Piper picked a peck of pickled
    peppers,
Where's the peck of pickled peppers
    Peter Piper picked?

Peter poked a poker at the piper, so the piper poked pepper at Peter.

Paul, please pause for proper applause.

Pass the pink peas please.

A pack of pesky pixies.
A pack of pesky pixies.
A pack of pesky pixies.

Plain bun, plum bun.
Plain bun, plum bun.
Plain bun, plum bun.

Please place the pleated pressed pants on the plain pressing plank.

Preshrunk shirts.
Preshrunk shirts.
Preshrunk shirts.

Please prune plum trees promptly.

Please prepare the paired pared pears near the unprepared pears near the pool.

Poor pure Pierre.
Poor pure Pierre.
Poor pure Pierre.

Pop bottles pop-bottles in pop shops;
The pop-bottles Pop bottles poor Pop drops.
When Pop drops pop-bottles, pop-bottles
  plop;
When pop-bottles topple, Pop mops slop.

     Peggy Babcock's mummy.
     Peggy Babcock's mummy.
     Peggy Babcock's mummy.

Picky pickpockets pick picked pockets.

Pretty poor peace prospects.

Is a pleasant peasant's pheasant present?

Pale pink plumage.
Pale pink plumage.
Pale pink plumage.

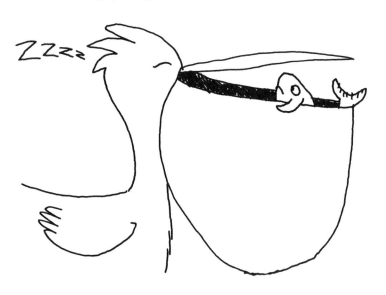

Pooped purple pelicans.
Pooped purple pelicans.
Pooped purple pelicans.

The quack quit asking quick questions.

The queen coined quick clipped quips.

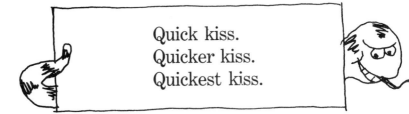

Quick kiss.
Quicker kiss.
Quickest kiss.

A right-handed fellow named Wright,
In writing "write" always wrote "rite"
  Where he meant to write right.
  If he'd written "write" right,
Wright would not have wrought rot writing
    "rite."

        A lump of red lead,
        A red lead lump.

Round and round the rugged rocks the ragged rascal ran.

Rex wrecks wet rocks.

Rubber baby-buggy bumpers.
Rubber baby-buggy bumpers.
Rubber baby-buggy bumpers.

Raise Ruth's red roof.
Raise Ruth's red roof.
Raise Ruth's red roof.

If rustlers wrestle wrestlers,
While rustlers rustle rustlers
Could rustlers rustle wrestlers
While wrestlers wrestle rustlers?

Rush the washing, Russell!

Six small slick seals.
Six small slick seals.
Six small slick seals.

Sherman shops at cheap chop suey shops.

Sheila seldom sells shelled shrimps.

She sells seashells by the seashore.

Selfish sharks sell shut shellfish.

Seth's sharp spacesuit shrank.

Mrs. Smith's Fish Sauce Shop.

Is Sherry's shortcake shop shut?
Is Shelly's shortstop shop shut?

She sells Swiss sweets.

Slick silk.
Slick silk.
Slick silk.

Does this shop stock shot silk shorts?

If she stops at the shop where I stop,
And if she shops at the shop where I shop,
Then I shan't stop to shop at the shop
Where she stops to shop.

Susie's shirt shop sells preshrunk shirts.

Sharon sews shocking shirts for soldiers.

The sad soldier should shoot soon.

Sharpshooters should shoot slowly.

Soldiers' shoulders shudder when shrill shells shriek.

Should six shaking soldiers share the shattered shield?

The short soldier shoots straight.

Sixty-six sick six-shooters.

Stagecoach stops.
Stagecoach stops.
Stagecoach stops.

Strange strategic statistics.
Strange strategic statistics.
Strange strategic statistics.

"Shoot, Sally!" shouted Slim Sam.

No shipshape ships shop stocks shop-soiled shirts.

"Sure, the ship's ship-shape, sir!"

Shallow sailing ships should shun shallow shoals.

The shallow ship showed signs of sinking.

Sixty-four swift sloops swing shorewards.

The sea ceaseth seething.
The sea ceaseth seething.
The sea ceaseth seething.

How many slim slimy snakes would slither silently to the sea if slim slimy snakes could slither silently?

### Smelts

Of all the smells I ever smelt,
I never smelt a smell that smelt
Like that smell I smelt smelled.

A selfish shellfish smelt a stale fish.
If the stale fish was a smelt,
Then the selfish shellfish smelt a smelt.

Should a shad, shelling shrimps for a shark,
Cease to shuck the shamed shrimps, who
    remark,
  "Serve us not without dressing!
  'Tis really distressing!"
Or should he just shuck the shrimps in the
    dark?

No shark shares swordfish steak.

### Swim!

Swim, Sam, swim,
Show them you're a swimmer!
Six sharp sharks seek small snacks,
So swim, Sam, swim!

Swan swam over the sea;
Swim, Swan, swim!
Swan swam back again;
Well swum, Swan!

## Shy Sheep

Some say shy shippers ship shy sheep.

Six shy shavers sheared six shy sheep.

Shameless shepherds shampoo shy sheep.

The sixth sheik's sixth sheep's sick.

### Shorn Sheep

Six sick shorn sheep.

BRRRRRRR!

Shorn sheep shouldn't sleep in a shack.
Shorn sheep should sleep in a shed.

## Silly Shoes

The shady shoe shop shows sharp sharkskin shoes.

Sharp sharkskin shoes.
Sharp sharkskin shoes.
Sharp sharkskin shoes.

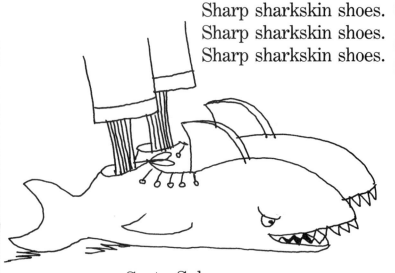

Sooty Sukey
Shook some soot
From sister Susie's
Sooty shoes.

The shrewd shrew's suede shoes.

Sid's shabby silver shoes still shine.

Showy sashes in a shut sash shop.

Such a shapeless sash!
Such a shapeless sash!
Such a shapeless sash!

Shoes and socks shock Susan.

The suitor wore shorts and a short shooting
    suit to a short shoot.
But the shorts didn't suit the short shooting
    suit,
And at the short shoot the short shooting
    suit didn't suit.
Oh, shoot!

Sally Swim saw Sadie Slee
Slowly, sadly swinging.
"She seems sorrowful," said she.
So she started singing.
Sadie smiled, soon swiftly swung;
Sitting straight, steered swiftly.
"See," said Sally, "something sung
Scatters sunshine swiftly!"

I went into my garden to slay snails.
I saw my little sister slaying snails.
I said, "Hello, my little sister, are you
    slaying snails?
If you slay snails, please slay small snails."

Surely the sun shall shine soon.

Some shun summer sunshine.

Shirley Simms shrewdly shuns sunshine and sleet.

The sun shines on the shop signs.

Sloppy shortstops.
Sloppy shortstops.
Sloppy shortstops.

Shabby soldiers shovel soft snow slowly.

Sneaky thieves seized the skis.

### Slick Ski Slopes

Sloppy skiers slide on slick ski slopes.

Sick cattle slip on slick ski slopes.

If he slipped, should she slip?

Sleepy Joe of snowy Stowe
Slid swiftly into action.
  Aboard his sled
  Away he sped,
He's sleeping now, in traction.

Through rifts in the lofts,
The soft snow sifts.
Then the white sheet lifts
And the wind packs drifts.

"Go, my son, and shut the shutter,"
This I heard a mother mutter.
"Shutter's shut," the boy did mutter,
"I can't shut'er any shutter."

Should she shut summer shutters slowly or
should she shut summer shutters swiftly?

The old school scold
Sold the school coal scuttle;
If the old school scold sold
The school coal scuttle,
The school should scold
And scuttle the old school scold.

I had an old saw,
And I bought a new saw.
I took the handle off the old saw
And put it on the new saw.
And of all the saws
I ever saw,
I never saw a saw saw
Like that new saw sawed.

Scams, stings and skulduggery.
Scams, stings and skulduggery.
Scams, stings and skulduggery.

Mr. See and Mr. Soar were old friends. See owned a saw and Soar owned a seesaw. Now See's saw sawed Soar's seesaw before Soar saw See, which made Soar sore. Had Soar seen See's saw before See saw Soar's seesaw, then See's saw would not have sawed Soar's seesaw. But See saw Soar's seesaw before Soar saw See's saw so See's saw sawed Soar's seesaw. It was a shame to let See see Soar so sore because See's saw sawed Soar's seesaw.

Down the slippery slide they slid
Sitting slightly sideways;
Slipping swiftly, see them skid
On holidays and Fridays.

Sixty-six sticky skeletons.
Sixty-six sticky skeletons.
Sixty-six sticky skeletons.

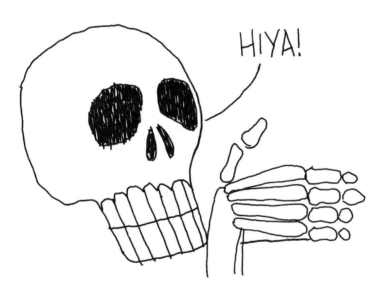

Amidst the mists and coldest frosts
With barest wrists and stoutest boasts
He thrusts his fists against the posts
And still insists he sees the ghosts.

A ghost's sheets would soon shrink in such
suds.

She shrieks as she stitches sheets.

She shall sew a slit sheet shut.

The sly sheet slasher slashed sheets.

Should she sell sheer sheets or should she
sell shaggy shawls?

### Shaving—Shaving

Shawn shaves a short cedar shingle thin.

Should Shawn shave a short thin single cedar shingle thin or shave a short thin single cedar shingle thinner?

Shave six short saplings.

WHEW!
THAT WAS
A CLOSE
SHAVE!

Shouldn't sweet-scented shaving soap soothe sore skin?

Sometimes Sheila thinks such soft thoughts.

I snuff shop snuff.
Do you snuff shop snuff?

Seven sleek
sleepless
sleepers
seek sleep.

The slightly sloping shed slips.

The shaky shed sheds sheets of shale.

Does Steve still strew straw in the still straw stall?

If silly Sally will shilly-shally, shall silly Willy
willy-nilly shilly-shally too?

A skunk sat on a stump;
The skunk thunk the stump stunk,
But the stump thunk the skunk stunk.

A tutor who tooted a flute
Tried to tutor two tooters to toot.
  Said the two to the tutor,
  "Is it harder to toot
Or to tutor two tooters to toot!"

I shot three shy thrushes.

Thirty-three sly shy thrushes.
Thirty-three sly shy thrushes.
Thirty-three sly shy thrushes.

There goes one tough top cop!

Thrash the thickset thug!
Thrash the thickset thug!
Thrash the thickset thug!

The third thickset thug thinks.

I thought a thought
But the thought I thought I thought wasn't
    the thought I thought.
If the thought I thought I thought had been
    the thought I thought I thought,
I wouldn't have thought so much.

Do thick tinkers think?

Tea for the thin twin tinsmith.

He says that a two twice-twisted twine
twisted twice twists twice as tight as a one
once-twisted twine twisted twice. But I say
that a two twice-twisted twine twisted twice
does not twist as tight as a one once-twisted
twine twisted twice.

## Thistles

Theophilus Thistle, the successful thistle-
    sifter,
Sifted sixty thistles through the thick of his
    thumb.

Thick thistle sticks.
Thick thistle sticks.
Thick thistle sticks.

OUCH!

Six thick thistles stuck together.

A tree toad loved a she-toad
That lived up in a tree.
She was a three-toed tree toad,
But a two-toed toad was he.
The two-toed toad tried to win
The she-toad's friendly nod,
For the two-toed toad loved the ground
On which the three-toed tree toad trod.
But no matter how the two-toed tree
     toad tried,
He could not please her whim.
In her three-toed bower,
With her three-toed power,
The three-toed she-toad vetoed him.

Truly rural.
Truly rural.
Truly rural.

'Twixt six thick thumbs stick six thick sticks.

Thelma sings the theme song.

Twelve trim twin-track tapes.
Twelve trim twin-track tapes.
Twelve trim twin-track tapes.

Trill two true tunes to the troops.

Theo's throat throbs and thumps, thumps and throbs.

Ted threw Fred thirty-three free throws.

Three thick things.
Three thick things.
Three thick things.

Three free through trains.
Three free through trains.
Three free through trains.

Tacky tractor trailer trucks.
Tacky tractor trailer trucks.
Tacky tractor trailer trucks.

An undertaker undertook to undertake an undertaking. The undertaking that the undertaker undertook was the hardest undertaking the undertaker ever undertook to undertake.

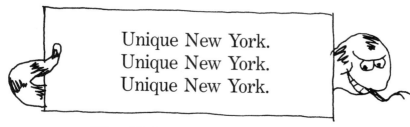

Unique New York.
Unique New York.
Unique New York.

The U.S. twin-screw cruiser.
The U.S. twin-screw cruiser.
The U.S. twin-screw cruiser.

What veteran ventriloquist whistles?

Valuable valley villas.
Valuable valley villas.
Valuable valley villas.

The wretched witch watched a walrus
washing.
Did the wretched witch watch a walrus
washing?
If the wretched witch watched a walrus
washing,
Where's the washing walrus the wretched
witch watched?

Which rich wicked witch wished the wicked
    wish?

If two witches watched two watches, which
    witch would watch which watch?

Which wristwatch is a Swiss wristwatch?

Real wristwatch straps.
Real wristwatch straps.
Real wristwatch straps.

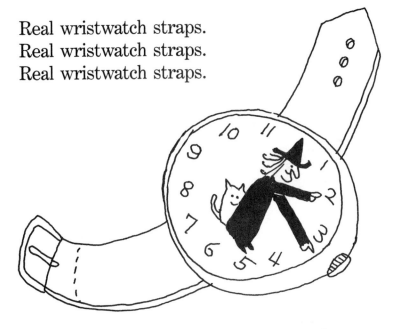

I wish I hadn't washed this wristwatch.
I washed all the wheels and the works.
Since this wristwatch got all washed,
Oh, how it jumps and jerks!

Billy Wood said he would carry the wood
through the woods, and if Wood said he
would, Wood would.

How much wood would a woodchuck chuck
If a woodchuck could chuck wood?
He would chuck the wood as much as he
        could
If a woodchuck could chuck wood.

Wilson whittles well-whittled wood whittle
by whittle.

If a warmly warbling warbler warbles to another warmly warbling warbler, which warmly warbling warbler warbles warmest?

Wetter leather never weathered wetter weather better.

Whether the weather be fine
Or whether the weather be not;
Whether the weather be cold
Or whether the weather be hot;
We'll weather the weather
Whatever the weather,
Whether we like it or not.

Wally Winkle wriggles his white, wrinkled
wig.

Which wishy-washy washerwoman wants to
watch?

War-weary warriors.
War-weary warriors.
War-weary warriors.

X-mas wrecks perplex and vex.

X-ray checks clear chests.

Ex-disk jockey.          The ex-egg examiner.
Ex-disk jockey.          The ex-egg examiner.
Ex-disk jockey.          The ex-egg examiner.

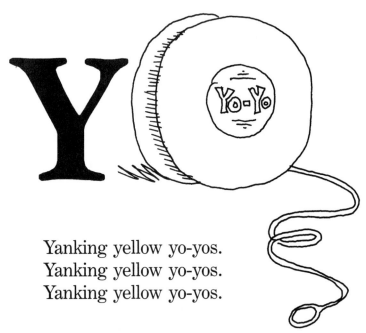

Yanking yellow yo-yos.
Yanking yellow yo-yos.
Yanking yellow yo-yos.

Yellow leather, yellow feather.
Yellow leather, yellow feather.
Yellow leather, yellow feather.

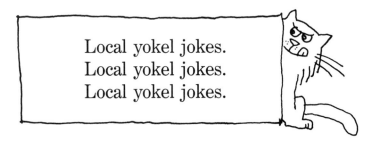

Local yokel jokes.
Local yokel jokes.
Local yokel jokes.

This is a zither.
Is this a zither?

Zizzi's zippy zipper zips.

Zithers slither slowly south.

# Index